Pastoring the Small Church

Pastoring the Small Church

*Remaining Faithful
in a Big Church World*

ERIC W. MOORE

RESOURCE *Publications* • Eugene, Oregon

PASTORING THE SMALL CHURCH
Remaining Faithful in a Big Church World

Copyright © 2013 Eric W. Moore. All rights reserved. Except for brief quotations in critical publications or reviews, no part of this book may be reproduced in any manner without prior written permission from the publisher. Write: Permissions, Wipf and Stock Publishers, 199 W. 8th Ave., Suite 3, Eugene, OR 97401.

Resource Publications
An Imprint of Wipf and Stock Publishers
199 W. 8th Ave., Suite 3
Eugene, OR 97401
www.wipfandstock.com

ISBN 13: 978-1-62564-294-3
Manufactured in the U.S.A.

Scripture quotations are taken from the NEW AMERICAN STANDARD BIBLE®, Copyright © 1960, 1962, 1963, 1968, 1971, 1972, 1973, 1975, 1977, 1995 by The Lockman Foundation. Used by permission.

To Marilyn, my wife and best friend

Faithful is he who calls you, and he also will bring it to pass.

—1 Thessalonians 5:24

Contents

Preface ix
Acknowledgments xi
Introduction: Megachurch World xiii

1 Whatcha Running? 1

2 Shh! Don't Tell Anyone! 9

3 Nice People 16

4 The Perfect Storm 22

5 Twist and Shout! 28

6 You Are Not the Church 33

7 Mirror, Mirror, On the Wall . . . 39

8 Delight Yourself in the Lord 45

9 Bring the Rain 51

Epilogue 57
Bibliography 59

Preface

This book is for the pastor of the small church: for the individuals who pastor the majority of the churches in the United States and around the world. These are the pastors who oversee a flock of 300 people or less. They have a significant amount of issues that the larger churches don't have, and therefore popular authors do not address them. As a matter of fact, you can visit any bookstore and see books by authors who pastor churches of two thousand, five thousand, ten thousand or more. Many of the solutions they offer and the ways they address issues do not apply to the pastor of a church of 150 people. This book is for the small church pastor. Hopefully as you read this, some of the challenges, issues, struggles and concerns that you have will be addressed and you will be encouraged in your walk with the Lord.

Acknowledgments

As in any endeavor, there are a number of people who work behind the scenes to make a project successful. I want to thank a few of those people.

First, I want to thank my wife, Marilyn, for her unswerving trust in the Lord, and in me. Without her support and patience, this project would never have gotten off the ground. I want to thank my children, Chanel, Samuel and Christina for allowing me the time that could have been spent with them to focus on this writing. God has blessed me with a wonderful family. I could not ask for more.

I want to thank Tree of Life Bible Fellowship Church for allowing me to serve as their pastor, and Sid and Joyce Jones who began this journey with me to plant the church several years ago. It has been an exciting one.

Many thanks to Dr. J. Brian Tucker for regularly challenging me to put my thoughts on paper. Thanks to Laura Evoe for applying her editing skills to the manuscripts.

A great deal of gratitude goes to my extended family and friends. I want to thank my parents, Charley and Evelyn, for their encouragement. Thanks to Brian and Fannie Moore for their on-going support.

Finally, I want to thank my Lord and Savior, Jesus Christ, for the opportunity to encourage others who are faithfully leading God's smaller flocks.

Introduction: Megachurch World

A MEGACHURCH IS DEFINED as a church where two thousand or more people attend the weekend worship service(s). In the 1900s, there were only ten megachurches in the United States. By 1970, there were only fifty. However, in 1980, there were 150 megachurches in America. By 1990, that number had doubled to 310, and in 2000 it had doubled once more to six hundred. By 2005, there were over 1,200 megachurches in America.[1]

Is all this growth the result of God's Spirit moving within His church, or is this the result of a cultural shift in our country? The truth is, it is probably a little of both. If we trace the growth of certain consumer industries, we will find that the megachurch phenomenon closely follows the consumer product world. For instance, Home Depot® was founded in 1978 in Atlanta, Georgia, and has come to be known as the fastest growing retailer in U.S. history.[2] A similar growth pattern can be seen with Costco®, which first opened in Seattle in 1983,[3] and of course Sam's Club® was also started in 1983 by Sam Walton in Midwest City,

---

1. Thumma and Travis, *Beyond Megachurch Myths*, 7.
2. Home Depot®, *Our Company: History*. Home Depot.
3. Lenora Chu, "Priced to grow: How Costco® got started," *CNN Money*.

Introduction: Megachurch World

Oklahoma.[4] What do all three of these companies have in common? They are considered "one-stop shops." They are a large physical location where the consumer can purchase multiple products ranging from home improvement to groceries to tires. They are a consumer's dream! No more does a person have to run all over town to purchase tires at the tire shop, groceries at the grocery store and lumber at the hardware store. Now, the consumer can travel to one place where all of their needs are met with one trip.

We see a similar phenomenon in the megachurch. It is a great place to come because the attendee is able to worship while the kids enjoy themselves. Megachurches usually have multiple worship services with multiple worship styles. Every family member can have his or her felt needs met under one roof on one campus, or under multiple roofs on multiple campuses. Megachurches also usually have a first class nursery where infants can be cared for and parents's worries about their children's well-being can be alleviated.

However, in the midst of the church growth movement, from 1990 to 2006, we find that the percentage of Christians attending church on any given Sunday has declined compared to the population growth in America.[5] According to David T. Olson,

> The American church is growing fastest in zip codes that are more affluent . . . Evangelical churches, in particular, are growing in suburbs that are home to affluent, educated residents. The median income in Lake Forest, California, home of Saddleback Community Church, is $78,681, more than $25,000 higher than the national median. In South Barrington, Illinois,

---

4. Sam's Club®, *About Us: History,* Sam's Club®.

5. Olson, *American Church in Crisis*, 35.

Introduction: Megachurch World

home of Willow Creek Community Church, the median income is more than $200,000 a year.[6]

So then, what happens in not-so-affluent areas? What happens in rural, small town, large town, and inner city America? Who ministers there? Often, it is a small-church pastor who does not have the finances or the resources that are needed to produce or sustain a megachurch.

Shoppers like the convenience of Costco or Sam's Club over the old grocery chains. However, a local grocery store in my community continues to thrive. The reason? It continues to meet the needs in our community. There is no sign of it going out of business anytime soon. The local hardware store in our community also continues to thrive, even though there is a Home Depot four miles away. I have been to both stores, yet when I am trying to find a specific fixture for my bathroom, I usually find it at the local store, and not at Home Depot. Our local hardware store's strategy is not to be the largest hardware store in the community; its strategy is to serve the people in the community with its unique needs.

Many have predicted the demise of the small church; however, I do not see it happening. The small church is *here to stay*. It belongs to Christ. We need more small church pastors with a strategy and a heart to reach communities that the megachurch will not be able to reach effectively. Once again, this book is written to encourage the small church pastor *not to give up*, but to know that you are a key piece of God's universal church and a key part of his strategy for reaching people for Jesus Christ.

Let's begin.

---

6. Ibid., 82.

1

Whatcha Running?

"I again saw under the sun that the race is not to the swift . . ."
—ECCLESIASTES 9:11A

DURING MY COLLEGE YEARS, I had a 1969 Camaro. I bought it for three hundred dollars, and spent all summer using my hard-earned money to fix it up and to make it look good. I bought new rims, new tires, and put headers on the exhaust system. I replaced the old carburetor with a Holley® brand high performance carburetor. My stereo was state of the art. The worn out shocks were upgraded to the expensive air shocks that lifted the rear end high enough to get a nosebleed. To make it look even better, I tossed the big steering wheel and replaced it with a 7-inch diameter wheel, and I replaced the carpet with blue bathroom plush carpet of the day. The old paint was stripped, and new midnight blue metallic flake paint was applied with an additional coat of clear. As I told my buddies, a fly couldn't land on the car without slipping and breaking its neck.

This car was my pride and joy.

One of the questions that the real hot-rodders (I was a wannabe) would ask is, "Whatcha running?" to see if I was "all show and no go." In essence, they wanted to know what was under the hood. This question was always posed before they asked me if I wanted to race. Of course, I always had a reason why today was not a good day to race. Actually, no day was a good day.

This is what I thought the phrase, "Whatcha running?" meant, that is, until I began pastoring a church. Those of us who are pastors of a small church understand what "Whatcha running?" really means.

It is a phrase that pastors use when they get together and start the small talk. The comparison begins after the initial greetings and pleasantries in order to size up one another. As we have our conversation, inevitably someone says "Whatcha Running?"—that translates into, "How many people do you have attending on Sunday morning?"

Unfortunately, we are evaluated upon how many people we have in the seats. Inevitably, those of us who are not "running" as much as others want to include everybody in the count: the dads, moms, children, pets, dolls and anything else that we can claim as something that fills the seats. I have often wondered why that question sends a chill down my spine, and why it causes so much anxiety in my heart. Is it because I measure my self-worth as a pastor by how many people attend our church? No doubt there are many small-church pastors who feel the same way. They are faithful in preaching, faithful in outreach, faithful in trying to minster to their people, have read all the books, and gone to all the seminars. They have tried to do everything that the Christian marketing masters have told them to do, and yet,

Whatcha Running?

they find out that they are not "running" what they thought they should.

Of course, inevitably this causes discouragement when one has put their heart and soul into the ministry and the results are not what they anticipated they should be. Not only do they receive discouragement from other pastors, but also discouragement from well-wishers. Have you noticed how often well-wishers also want to know "Whatcha running?" They don't use that phrase. They just ask, "How many people attend your church?"

How do you respond to that? Is it how many people are there on Easter? How many people are there on Christmas? How many people are there on Mother's Day? Or how many people are there in the midst of the summer when everybody's on vacation and it is just you and two other people in the church: one of them is your wife and the other is your kid?

"Whatcha running?"

It seems that whatever number you give is never large enough. After you have done the calculation in your head of adding the total attendance for the year and dividing it by the 52 Sundays of the year, subtracting the outliers of the high and low Sundays as to not eschew the statistical results for the purpose of plotting an accurate bell curve of results. When you give the most accurate number you can, it is always followed by a kind smile and statement, "Don't worry, I'm sure it will grow."

The metrics for growing a church are normally listed as the ABCs of church growth. The letter A stands for attendance, B stands for building(s), and C stands for cash. You can peruse any Christian bookstore and read some of the more popular church growth authors and you will see an emphasis (or over-emphasis) on attendance. The popular authors encourage us to spread a broad net to bring in all the people that we can. This is for the purpose of reaching them for Jesus Christ. If we are successful in bringing in many people, then we find ourselves in a situation where we either need to increase the number of worship services or enlarge our building. Either of these options shows that we are a successful church. Of course, the more that we have in attendance, the more money is given to the ministry and the more that we are able to do for the Kingdom of God.

All of this sounds extremely spiritual, and it probably is, but it usually does not work for the small church pastor. The pastor of a small church has probably tried a number of evangelistic efforts to little or no avail. The building that he uses is probably old and in need of repair. The budget does not change much from year to year, because the same people that were giving last year will be the same people giving this year. No wonder he is discouraged when he runs into church pastors whose churches are growing by 10–25 percent per year, with an increasing budget and building expansions. We have all heard it, "If it is healthy, it should be growing." So what is the problem?

I would like to propose an additional letter to the ABC's of church growth: letter D for Depth or spiritual growth. Often (but not always), the churches that are effective at doing letters A, B and C are not doing a great job at letter D. On the other hand, small churches have the greatest opportunity for spiritual growth. In many respects, they have the small group community that many of the large churches are trying to emulate.

Large churches have their share of challenges. Two of these areas are living in genuine community and discipleship. In the book entitled, *Move*, Bill Hybels states,

> 18 percent of our congregation—more than 1,000 people—had stalled spiritually and didn't know what to do about it. Many were consider-

> ing leaving. And some of our most mature and fired up Christians wanted to go deeper in their faith and be challenged more but felt as if our church wasn't helping them get to the next level.[1]

One of the advantages of a small church is the close contact that the pastor has with his sheep. Community and discipleship emanate out of the small church.

I am reminded of a few select passages in Paul's first letter to the Thessalonians. Usually we go to chapters four and five of 1 Thessalonians for the purpose of explaining the eschatological events regarding the Rapture and the Day of the Lord. However, in doing that, we often miss the purpose for which Paul wrote concerning those events. In 1 Thessalonians 4:13-17, Paul gives the details regarding the Rapture, but in verse 18 of that same chapter, he tells the Thessalonians, "Therefore comfort one another with these words." In chapter five, he continues to explain the events regarding the Day of the Lord. When he gets to verse 11, he tells them "Therefore, encourage one another and build up one another." He continues on in verse 13 of the same chapter telling them to "live in peace with one another." In verse 15, he tells them to seek after that which is "good for one another."

As you can see, there are a number of verses with regards to the body ministering to the body. Ministry happens in close-knit relationships. Generally, people have to know one another in order to minister to one another effectively. This is where the small church has its advantage: real community happens in small groups. Once again, the small church by definition is a small group.

As pastors, our challenge is to get the small church to look outward, while not getting discouraged with the poor results. The small church has been criticized for being

1. Hawkins and Parkinson, *Move*, 9.

ingrown and introspective rather than missional, but that doesn't have to be the case. Real spiritual growth will include outreach to the community. The goal of the small church pastor is to lead his people to live with the tension of the needs of the body of Christ and the needs of the masses. Both are important to the Lord.

I love the first three chapters of the Book of Revelation. I've heard my share of sermons on the church of Ephesus and the church of Laodicea. I am amazed at how often non-large church people will automatically associate the church of Laodicea with large churches. "See, pastor, large churches are condemned by God for relying on their resources." I am intrigued by this form of biblical interpretation. Hopefully, they didn't learn this from one of my sermons. In my experience, God has used large, Christ-centered churches to be a great source of support. I believe God raises up large, medium and small churches to His glory. However, small churches (and their pastors) can have an inferiority complex if they are not careful. This should not be.

Whenever this inferiority complex begins to creep into my thoughts, I remind myself of the church of Philadelphia in the Book of Revelation. There is something intriguing about this church. Jesus stated,

> 7 And to the angel of the church in Philadelphia write: He who is holy, who is true, who has the key of David, who opens and no one will shut, and who shuts and no one opens, says this: 8 'I know your deeds. Behold, I have put before you an open door which no one can shut, because you have a little power, and have kept My word, and have not denied My name.'

Although this church had "a little power," God had opened a door that nobody could shut. Let me repeat this in case you just drifted. God had *opened a door that no person could shut* because this church had little power, and had remained faithful to the Lord. Is this not the plight of the small church? We have so few resources, so little influence and so little power. Yet if we remain faithful, God opens doors that no one can close.

It is of interest that of the seven churches listed in chapters two and three of the Book of Revelation, Philadelphia is one of only two churches that the Lord does not rebuke. It is the church without power that the Lord commends. In fact, He tells them to "hold fast what you have, so that no one will take your crown;" (3:7). There is a crown for the church (and pastor) without power if they continue to depend upon God.

One day I was explaining to one of my friends, who leads a large church, how we had found ourselves in a financial bind. We didn't have the money to pay our lease. It was not our fault; the money just was not there. What did we do? We cried out to God in prayer, and it went something like this: "Lord you know our plight. You are the One who ordained this ministry. We do not have the money to pay the rent. However, nothing is too hard for you. You own cattle on a thousand hills. What is this small amount to you? Please provide!" That evening, God provided. When I told my buddy this story, he replied, "I envy you. When you find yourself in trouble, you pray. When we find ourselves in a bind, we throw money at it."

There is something to be said about our church being dependent upon the Lord. It reminds us that our help comes from him. With our little strength, we have sent missions support all around the world. We have been involved in local and global missions. We have provided for the poor and fed the hungry. We continually reach out to our community. We might not be able to do it like the "big boys," but

I think we are doing okay. All of what we have been able to accomplish has only been by God's grace.

The question is not, "Whatcha running?" it is "How ya running?" As long as we are running with the Lord, that is all that really matters.

2

Shh! Don't Tell Anyone!

"Three may keep a secret, if two of them are dead."
—Benjamin Franklin

When I was twelve years old, my parents finally bought my brother and I a dog. His name was Champ. Champ was a mutt. He was part German-Shepherd, part Alaskan Husky and part Golden Retriever, among other things. We only had Champ for about six months before one of my neighbors purchased a German-Shepherd. Unlike Champ, his dog was a pure bred. This meant nothing to me. I didn't know what the phrase "pure bred" meant. However, we had a mutual friend who did. This mutual friend called me shortly after my neighbor purchased his pup. He wondered, "Why would my neighbor's parents purchase a German-Shepherd like mine? Why would they purchase a pure bred?" He asked, "Why are they trying to complete with you?" They never had a desire to purchase a dog before you got one."

I honestly had never thought about those things before. However, our mutual friend seemed to make some good points. So I agreed with his insightful reasoning. I told him, "It didn't make sense to me." I even added to his logic. I stated, "They probably won't take care of their dog anyway." Shortly after this statement, the conversation ended.

The next day, my neighbor would not talk to me. I didn't know exactly why; however, I figured it had something to do with the conversation I had with our mutual friend. I was correct in my assumption. It seems that our mutual friend had another person listening on the telephone line. Together they verified to my neighbor that I had bad mouthed him and his dog.

Wow! I wasn't expecting that! I learned my lesson. I need to be very careful with whom I share secrets. I can't trust people. I need to keep my thoughts to myself.

Most people may not have had my exact experience, but they've had a similar experience. They've been hurt by someone they trust. They have also made a decision to protect themselves because of it. In other words, they have decided that they don't need any close friends. Unfortunately, this is a key factor of prolonged disillusionment.

Disillusionment has to deal with the realization that one is not where he thought he would be at a particular point in time. Usually this does not affect the younger pastors, but more or less the middle-age pastors or those nearing middle age. However, younger pastors and leaders are not immune to this "malaise." This phenomenon can happen when an individual evaluates where he is in his personal ministry and realizes that he is not where he thought he would be. You can see what affect this has on him, or at least you can understand why this has an effect on him. According to one source, 90 percent of pastors feel they are inadequately trained to cope with ministry demands, and it was completely different from what they anticipated before entering the ministry.[1]

Those of us who have grown up in the United States were told that if we go to college, then go on to Graduate School, get good grades and be in the proper field of study we would get a decent job. Somehow, we have also appropriated that into ministry. Many of us have gone to Bible College or Seminary, some even on to obtain doctorate degrees. As a result of all this Christian education, we secretly think that we are entitled to a wonderful pastorate or ministry, when that is the furthest thing from the truth.[2]

Christian ministry is nothing like the secular world. There are those who are involved in ministry who really don't have much of a formal Bible education, and there are others who have extensive formal Bible education and yet find themselves not in ministry at all.[3] I have addressed this concern with several of my seminary students. Students will look at some of the professors, see the degrees they have and say, "Well, if I can just get these degrees, I know that the sky is the limit." Unfortunately, some of these same students will graduate with a seminary degree and find out that not many people, organizations or churches are really interested in them. And of course, here comes the disillusionment.

It is the same way as a pastor; you've come to lead a small church, you've been called, the people seem to be excited about your gifts, your skill set, and your education.

1. Jim Fuller, "10 Reasons Why Pastors Leave the Ministry," Pastoral Care, Inc.

2. For example, on February 27, 2012 the US News and World Report website lists the top 10 best jobs in 2012: Jada Graves, "The Best Jobs of 2012," US News and World Report.

3. Jim Cymbala of Brooklyn Tabernacle is an example of a pastor who has led a dynamic church for a number of years and does not hold a Bible college or Seminary degree.

Pastoring the Small Church

After pastoring for a period of time you realize that all these dreams, hopes and aspirations for this ministry are not being realized. This is when disillusionment sets in. Unfortunately, admitting disillusionment with one's ministry is often viewed as a "taboo." If we talk about the fact that we are disillusioned with our personal ministry or our walk with the Lord, then we are seen as less than spiritual. We think that we cannot talk about it since we are the leader and others are looking to us for spiritual direction. We are the ones who are supposed to keep the faith at all times.

When we find ourselves in the valley, how do we respond? How do we address this? How do we get out of this?

When I find myself in this disillusioned state of mind, I turn to Psalm 73. It is in this Psalm that Asaph expresses exactly how he feels about his predicament. I love the fact that he doesn't hold back his feelings from God.

> Surely God is good to Israel, to those who are pure in heart. 2 But as for me, my feet had almost slipped; I had nearly lost my foothold; (Psalm 73:1–2)

Asaph knows that God is good to Israel and those who follow after God with a pure heart. Theologically, he is sure of this truth. However, his personal experience does not seem to line up with what he theologically knows to be true. He confesses that he almost lost his grip on his ministry and walk with the Lord. Maybe you can relate to Asaph's plight?

He continues,

> 3 For I envied the arrogant when I saw the prosperity of the wicked. 4 They have no struggles; their bodies are healthy and strong. 5 They are free from the burdens common to man; they are not plagued by human ills. 6 Therefore pride is their necklace; they clothe themselves with violence. 7 From their callous hearts comes iniquity;

the evil conceits of their minds know no limits. 8 They scoff, and speak with malice; in their arrogance they threaten oppression. 9 Their mouths lay claim to heaven, and their tongues take possession of the earth. 10 Therefore their people turn to them and drink up waters in abundance. 11 They say, "How can God know? Does the Most High have knowledge?" 12 This is what the wicked are like—always carefree, they increase in wealth; (Psalm 73:3–12).

Asaph, like us, began to look at those around him that were not living for God. He surmised that their life was much easier and more pleasant than his. Some of these individuals even mocked the God he served and yet, they didn't suffer like him.

Have you ever felt like that? You have turned your back on the world to serve Jesus and yet, there doesn't seem to be much of a payoff down here. Don't get me wrong, we know that there will be a reward in heaven; however, it would be nice to receive some fringe benefits on this side of eternity, especially since we are serving him. Didn't Jesus say, "Seek first the kingdom of God and all these things would be added to you?"[4] So where are these things?

Let's be honest with each other. It is very difficult to live in the United States of America and not be daily bombarded by the financial and material success of others. After a while, we are all tempted to wonder, "Where is my little piece of the pie?" This was Asaph's dilemma.

He felt like us,

> 13 Surely in vain have I kept my heart pure; in vain have I washed my hands in innocence; (Psalm 73:13).

---

4. Matthew 6:33

Pastoring the Small Church

Do you know what is funny? Right now you probably want to tell Asaph to "Pull it together, dude. It is not that bad." Right? You want to put on your ministerial hat, coat or robe and theologically give him a lecture on God's goodness. However, Asaph already knows that. He knows it, just like we already know it. However, when we are going through it no amount of theological niceties is going to resolve the issue. It is just how we "feel" at the moment. We need to have our pity party with God. We need to voice our sincere disillusionment with our circumstances. God already knows where we are. It is we who need to come to grips with it.

One of Asaph's major issues was his inability to share his concerns with others. He states,

> 14 All day long I have been plagued; I have been punished every morning. 15 If I had said, "I will speak thus," I would have betrayed your children. 16 When I tried to understand all this, it was oppressive to me; (Psalm 73:14–16).

Don't run to verse 17 too quickly. Asaph's struggle is highlighted in these two verses. He has had an internal struggle raging for some time. Being the worship leader, he felt that he could not voice his struggles for fear of discouraging those under his leadership. At the same time, he was torturing himself by trying to resolve the issue on his own.

This happens to current-day ministry leaders as well. As a seminary professor, I have been absolutely amazed at how many pastors and Christian leaders do not have genuine friends. When I say friends, I am not talking about acquaintances or denominational associates. I am talking about genuine friends with whom we can share our inner most struggles. Somewhere, somehow a lie has been perpetrated. That lie is that the Christian leader doesn't need friends and that ministry and service will substitute for friendships. I hope that pin was sharp enough to burst your

Shh! Don't Tell Anyone!

bubble. We all need Christian friends to help us through these times of disillusionment. I have two male friends in my life that I can call at any time of the day and night and share my struggles, problems and issues. Do you have that? We all need friends in our life.

As we look back at verse 17, we see that in addition to needing genuine friends, Asaph needed a fresh view of God. He stated that he struggled,

> 17 till I entered the sanctuary of God; then I understood their final destiny; (Psalm 73:17).

When Asaph entered the sanctuary he got a fresh perspective on his struggle. These people that he envied would soon be no more. However, what he was doing would last eternally. Asaph went into the sanctuary and received a new perspective. The text doesn't say, but I don't think Asaph went into the sanctuary to lead worship. It was leading worship that caused his disillusionment in the first place. He probably entered the sanctuary alone to meet with God.

For some of us, that is what we need more than anything. We need time alone with God. We need time away from the ministry. We need time to hear God's voice again and be reminded why we are in ministry. We need to sense his leading and promptings in our heart again.

PRACTICAL APPLICATIONS

If you find yourself in the land of disillusionment, why don't you consider doing the following?

1. Renew (or develop) at least one friendship with a person you can trust.
2. Schedule two consecutive Sundays off from ministry. Go on a personal retreat to fall back in love with God. Trust me, the church will survive without you being there.

3

Nice People

"Blessed is he who expects nothing, for he shall never be disappointed."

—Alexander Pope

In Kenneth Boa's book, *Conformed to His Image*, he lists five different types of Christians: Very Resourceful People (VRP); Very Important People (VIP); Very Trainable People (VTP); Very Nice People (VNP); and Very Dependent People (VDP).[1] Those five types can also be broken into two separate groups as well. As pastors, the VRPs, VIPs and VTPs are people that we do ministry with. The VNPs and VDPs are the people we do ministry to.

It seems that a significant number of people who end up in small churches are "nice people." Small churches tend to have people who are very nice and kind. Most show up at least two Sundays a month. They are very helpful when they arrive. They often take notes on the sermon. A segment of

1. Boa, *Conformed to His Image*, 48–49.

Nice People

them come to Bible Study and Sunday School. They generally know the Bible and are generally eager to learn.

They learn for the purpose of making sure they are in right relationship with God. They learn so they will be able to raise their kids in the fear and admonition of the Lord. They learn so that God will continue to bless them. After all, they want to be good people, good citizens and good Christians. You could say they want to be the "salt of the earth." Their goal in life is be model Christian citizens who raise well rounded children who receive the best education and are exposed to every activity, sport, camp, hobby and contest known to mankind. Therefore, they have little or no time for doing the work of the ministry.

"Nice People" tend to not sacrifice for the ministry. They believe in a sense that it is the pastor's (clergy's) job to do that. Although it is not always stated, "nice people" often feel that is why they pay the pastor. When the "nice person" gives his offering, it is for the expressed purpose of the minister doing the work of the ministry. It has been said that the small church does not want a pastor, but a chaplain.[2] "Nice people" want chaplains.

As a small church pastor, you already know the dilemma that I am about to present, but humor me by continuing to read. Most small churches cannot afford to pay the pastor a full-time salary. So how can a part-time pastor do all "the work?" Most pastors of small churches have to work outside of their church.

If this is not enough, you pick up a book from the local bookstore by a well-known pastor of a large church who tells you that you should only be praying, studying and teaching God's Word. They will go as far as to imply that you are in sin if you do anything else. The truth is Paul worked, and Aquila and Pricilla worked with Paul. Most pastors in

2. Bierly, *How to Thrive as a Small-Church Pastor,* 41.

the third world work to provide for their family. The pastor of a small church will generally do what he needs to do to continue shepherding his flock. Can I get an "Amen" here?

No wonder pastors of small churches become disappointed with their flock. Since they do not have a paid pastoral staff, they have to depend upon their congregation to get things done. When their members continue to make excuses why they can't commit to overseeing a ministry or take the leadership role for a particular task, the pastor can get pretty disappointed in his people.

Worse than a member declining to lead a ministry is a member agreeing to lead a ministry and then deciding not to follow through at the last minute. Or better yet, a member agreeing and then disappearing until after the ministry is completed. I have been told that, "For some people, lying to the pastor is actually a form of honor."[3] Since the person does not want to disappoint the pastor (to his face), she lies so that she can disappoint him later. Can I be candid? Either form stinks.

The pastor is also disappointed by the unhealthy choices of his members. After the pastor has spent hours of counseling to help remove a woman from an unhealthy relationship with an abusive man, she goes right back to the man after he says, "I'm sorry." Or how about the pastor who spends hours at the hospital praying and comforting a troubled teen just to have him return to his rebellious ways once he is released from the hospital. How often has the pastor of a small church said to himself, "How can he be so stupid?" (I know you would never say that so, I'm saying it for you).

The small church pastor has to learn to deal with constant disappointment. How does one do that? How does

3. A friend told this humorous, but truthful, insight to me. I'm still trying figure out if I should be laughing or crying.

Nice People

one continue to deal with disappointment week after week, month after month, and year after year and not find oneself getting bitter towards his or her members?

I believe some insight can be gained by looking at Matthew 26:36–46.

> 36 Then Jesus came with them to a place called Gethsemane, and said to His disciples, "Sit here while I go over there and pray." 37 And he took with him Peter and the two sons of Zebedee, and began to be grieved and distressed. 38 Then he said to them, "My soul is deeply grieved, to the point of death; remain here and keep watch with me." 39 And he went a little beyond *them*, and fell on his face and prayed, saying, "My Father, if it is possible, let this cup pass from me; yet not as I will, but as you will." 40 And he came to the disciples and found them sleeping, and said to Peter, "So, you *men* could not keep watch with me for one hour? 41 "Keep watching and praying that you may not enter into temptation; the spirit is willing, but the flesh is weak." 42 He went away again a second time and prayed, saying, "My Father, if this cannot pass away unless I drink it, your will be done." 43 Again he came and found them sleeping, for their eyes were heavy. 44 And he left them again, and went away and prayed a third time, saying the same thing once more. 45 Then he came to the disciples and said to them, "Are you still sleeping and resting? Behold, the hour is at hand and the Son of Man is being betrayed into the hands of sinners."

We see in this passage, Jesus took his inner circle, Peter, James and John, into the Garden of Gethsemane with him. It was time to pray. The moment for which Jesus came to this earth is at hand, and he wants his closest disciples to keep alert and be fervent in prayer. Surely they understand the gravity of the moment. They have spent three and a half years with him. They have to know that if there was ever a time that Jesus needed them, it was now! So what does Jesus find them doing after each of his three prayers? They are sleeping. Jesus states that his disciples are willing in spirit, but their flesh is weak.

So my question is, "If Jesus' closest disciples let him down, what makes us think that our congregants will not let us down?" Having pastored for a number of years, I am convinced that Jesus is more interested in conforming His shepherds into His image than the shepherd's sheep. Isaiah tells us that Jesus was a man of sorrows.[4] Disappointment seems to be one of the means by which God brings sorrows into our lives.

Therefore, we should be disappointed. But we should be disappointed for the right reasons. We should not be disappointed because things did not go our way. Nor should we be disappointed because our feelings have been hurt. We should be disappointed because we want the best for our flock and yet they don't want the best for themselves. This should drive us to prayer on their behalf.

One of my mentors once told me that often God would put something on his heart for the ministry. Then he would try to get someone to own it, but nobody would. He used to think that something was wrong with his people. Later he realized that something was wrong with him. He began to understand that God put the idea on his heart so that he would begin praying for it. It might take six months, a year or even two years, but eventually God would raise up someone who wanted to lead the same ministry, independent of his asking or prodding. Maybe some of our people keep disappointing us because we have confused God giving us

---

4. Isaiah 53:3

Nice People

something to pray about with needing to find a person to carry out the task.

One of the great things about the Gethsemane story is that it was not the end of the story for Peter, James and John. When we see them in the book of Acts, they have been transformed into new people. Keep praying. Jesus did not give up on His disciples. Neither should we give up on our people.

4

The Perfect Storm

"Although the sun is shining, it still feels like night"
—Anonymous

You probably remember the movie and book, "The Perfect Storm,"[1] which was based upon the true-life story in the Atlantic Ocean off the coast of Gloucester, Massachusetts. Billy Tyne was the captain of the sword fishing boat named, the Andrea Gail. By the fall of 1991, Billy and his crew had not landed a significant catch. In October, he decided to go out to sea one last time. Despite the warning of a possible storm on the horizon, he heads out to an area beyond the normal fishing grounds known as the Flemish Cap. It is there that they encounter three extreme weather fronts, which collided to produce what some have called, "The Perfect Storm." Unfortunately, the Andrea Gail was not able to

1. Junger, *The Perfect Storm,* 1997. This story was also made into a movie in the year 2000: *The Perfect Storm*, DVD, directed by Wolfgang Petersen (2000; Burbank, CA: Warner Home Video, 2004).

The Perfect Storm

escape the grips of the storm. Billy and his crew all died and the Andrea Gail was destroyed.

"The Perfect Storm" is the phrase I use to describe what can happen when the discouragement, disillusionment, and disappointment described in the first three chapters collide in a pastor's life. The result of the perfect storm can be depression. This is a real serious concern in the pastorate. Some studies state that as many as 70 percent of pastors constantly fight depression.[2] This may explain why so many pastors leave the ministry.

Over the last twenty years I have found myself struggling with depression due to ministry. I believe I understand the effects that depression can have on a person's life. Each time it occurred as a result of "the perfect storm."

About four years ago, my wife and I were having breakfast at one of our local hangouts. I decided to open up to her about the internal struggle I was having. I looked across the table into my wife's eyes and said, "Honey, I am depressed." I was looking for those warm, comforting words of "Oh, honey, I'm so sorry to hear that. What can I do to help you?" But the response was somewhat shocking. She said, "I know. As a matter of fact, our entire family knows. You've been depressed for about 3 months. I was wondering when you were going to talk about it." Whoa! I didn't expect that!

The truth is that we are only fooling ourselves. Those who are close to us know we are struggling with something. In fact, they are probably struggling right along with us. The statistics prove this to be the case. Our spouses struggle right along with us. One source reports the following statistics:

---

2. Maranatha Life's Life-Line For Pastors, "Statistics About Pastors," Maranatha Life.

Pastoring the Small Church

- 94 percent of clergy families feel the pressures of the pastor's ministry.
- 80 percent of spouses feel the pastor is overworked.
- 80 percent of spouses feel left out and underappreciated by church members.
- 80 percent of pastors' spouses wish their spouse would choose a different profession.
- 66 percent of church members expect a minister and family to live at a higher moral standard than themselves.[3]

Let me ask you a few questions. Has the joy of doing ministry left? Has the excitement dissipated? Is the enthusiasm gone? Do the colors in your world seem to be muted and drab? Then you are probably depressed or on your way there. You need to know that there is a way out, and that many saints of God have had bouts with depression. It is more common than you think. The perfect storm does not have to sink your ship.

Let's take a look at Jeremiah the prophet.

> 4 Now the word of the LORD came to me saying, 5 "Before I formed you in the womb I knew you, and before you were born I consecrated you; I have appointed you a prophet to the nations;"(Jeremiah 1:4–5).

God made it clear that he had called Jeremiah into the ministry, and Jeremiah knew that he had been called. God had called Jeremiah to speak to His people on His behalf.

Yet, twenty years into his ministry, he is wrestling with self-pity and depression. He states,

---

3. Pastoral Care, Inc., "Statistics in the Ministry," Pastoral Care, Inc.

> 14 Cursed be the day when I was born; Let the day not be blessed when my mother bore me! 15 Cursed be the man who brought the news to my father, saying, "A baby boy has been born to you!" And made him very happy. 16 But let that man be like the cities which the Lord overthrew without relenting, And let him hear an outcry in the morning and a shout of alarm at noon; 17 Because he did not kill me before birth, so that my mother would have been my grave, And her womb ever pregnant. 18 Why did I ever come forth from the womb to look on trouble and sorrow, So that my days have been spent in shame? (Jeremiah 20:14–18).

What happened? Yes, Jeremiah had a tough task of preaching to a rebellious nation. Yes, Jeremiah was continually criticized. Yes, Jeremiah was persecuted. But wasn't he "called" by God? Surely, he should not be depressed, right? Wrong! Jeremiah was human, just like the rest of us. The reason we are in ministry is because we have been "called." Being "called" does not make us exempt from bouts of depression.

Even the great English pastor and preacher, Charles Haddon Spurgeon, fought with depression, so you are in good company. On October 19, 1856, ten thousand people were crammed into the hall to hear Spurgeon preach, with another ten thousand outside. Not long after services began, someone yelled, "Fire!" The panic that followed caused the deaths of seven people. For several weeks pastor Spurgeon secluded himself in depression over the event.[4] However, it didn't stop his ministry.

Depression didn't stop Jeremiah either. God continued to provide for Jeremiah throughout his difficult ministry.

---

4. Amundsen, "The Anguish and Agonies of Charles Spurgeon," 23–35; Erroll Hulse and David Kingdon, eds., *A Marvelous Ministry*.

Fast-forward approximately eighteen years to the destruction of Jerusalem by the Babylonian empire. Jeremiah was the one person who found favor with the Babylonians.

> 2 Now the captain of the bodyguard had taken Jeremiah and said to him, "The Lord your God promised this calamity against this place; 3 and the Lord has brought it on and done just as He promised. Because you people sinned against the Lord and did not listen to His voice, therefore this thing has happened to you. 4 "But now, behold, I am freeing you today from the chains which are on your hands. If you would prefer to come with me to Babylon, come along, and I will look after you; but if you would prefer not to come with me to Babylon, never mind. Look, the whole land is before you; go wherever it seems good and right for you to go;" (Jeremiah 40:2–4).

Just as the Lord provided for Jeremiah, He will provide for you. The perfect storm may not pass quickly, but it will pass. You are valuable to the Lord. You have been given a tough assignment. However, just as the Lord was with Jeremiah during his tough times, He is with you.

Several years ago, our family went on a vacation in the Bahamas. One of the excursions was the opportunity to snorkel in the Caribbean Sea. A number of my family members and I put on our flippers, water vests, goggles and snorkel and began to swim along the surface of the water. As a result, we were able to see a number of different coral reefs and beautiful, colorful fish under the water. However, ever since that excursion, I've wondered how the environment is deeper under the water. Is it just as beautiful? Or, is this where the more unattractive, unappealing sea creatures reside? This may be analogous to our condition. For

The Perfect Storm

some of us, snorkeling along the surface of the water is fine, and depression hits us like a wave in the sea. As long as we continue to keep our wits about us, we can get through the wave. For others of us, we probably need to go deeper to where some unattractive issues lie. The depression that we feel because of ministry may not be what is actually causing the depression. A difficult ministry may be God's way of exposing issues in our heart and soul that need to be exposed and healed.

Consider this. If after prayer and confession with close friends, the depression does not subside, consider getting good biblical counseling from a trained professional. It could save your ministry and much more.

5

Twist and Shout!

*"There are short-cuts to happiness,
and dancing is one of them."*

—Vicki Baum

My parents had a lot of records. We listened to "Soul Man" by Sam and Dave,[1] "R-E-S-P-E-C-T" by Aretha Franklin[2] and "I heard it through the Grape Vine" by Marvin Gaye.[3] The one song we did not have but I loved listening to was, "Twist and Shout" by The Beatles.[4] When that song would come on the radio, my brother and I would begin doing

---

1. Isaac Hayes and David Porter, "Soul Man," Sam & Dave, *Soul Men*.

2. Otis Redding, "RESPECT," Aretha Franklin, *I Never Loved a Man The Way I Love You*.

3. Norman Whitfield and Barrett Strong, "I Heard It Through the Grapevine," Marvin Gaye, *In the Groove*.

4. Phil Medley and Bret Burns, "Twist and Shout," The Beatles, *Please Please Me*.

Twist and Shout!

the dance called "The Twist." Kids our age were often encouraged by adults to "twist." They wanted to see who could "twist" the best. Doing "the twist" was fun, but the best part for me was "the shout." The Beatles would sing, "Twist and Shout." Later in the song would come the climax—they would begin with "Ahhhhhhhhhh, Ahhhhhhhhhh, Ahhhhhhhhhh, Ahhhhhhhhhhh, Yeah!"[5] (You have to know the song). That was fun!

The song reminds me of what ministry *should* be. Let me explain. Many of us had no intention of ever being the pastor of a small church. I can honestly say as a small child, teen and young adult that it was the furthest thing from my mind. It was probably the furthest thing from yours as well. Somehow, from our human perspective, we stumbled into the pastorate of a small church. Yes, God called us. Yes, we thought we would be in ministry. Yes, we were excited about the possibilities and potential of pastoring, but we didn't see ourselves presiding over a small church.

But here we are. Once we arrived, we thought we could take the ministry from *here* to *there*. I don't know exactly where *there* is with regards to your ministry, but most small church pastors believe that their purpose is to lead the church from *here* and take them to *there*. However, after years of struggles, prayers and heartache, we find that the ministry is not *there,* but still *here*. And we are coming to the realization that the dream we had for the ministry is not being realized.

Well, it is time to twist and shout! You are probably exactly where God wants you. God does not want you to stop leading, but he is just looking to redirect you. As individuals, we naturally have dreams and a vision for the church that God has called us to pastor. However, the task that God

---

5. Ibid.

wants to accomplish within this church may be somewhat different from what we have envisioned.

I remember at a pastor's retreat, one individual asked me how our church was going. I said, "It is going pretty good except for the fact that we've been trying to accomplish this one thing for a number of years. No matter what we do, we have not been able to accomplish it." Then my friend said something that really made me think. He said, "What is God already doing in your ministry?" That question caused me to stop and ponder, "What *is* God already doing in our ministry?" The answer to that question revolutionized my view of the ministry with regards to our church.

Many of us would do good to stop driving our people to accomplish the mission we thought God gave us when we started pastoring our church and begin the process of understanding what God is already doing. His purpose for our pastorate is much bigger than us. It is time to twist and shout!

One of my favorite personalities of Scripture is John the Baptist. If there was anyone that knew his mission and purpose in life, it was John. It seems as if John knew his purpose before he was born. You remember when Mary, Jesus's mother, visited John's mother Elizabeth. When Elizabeth heard Mary's voice, John leaped in Elizabeth's womb. John knew that his purpose in life was to point people to Jesus and prepare the way for him.

John stated that he was to decrease and Jesus was to increase.[6] In other words, it was not about John, it was all about Jesus! John was baptizing people in the Jordan River for the remission of sins. He was exhorting people to repent of their sins. This was his purpose in life and ministry.

However, something unexpected happened in Matthew chapter 3. Jesus comes to John in order to be baptized.

6. John 3:30.

Twist and Shout!

Matthew 3:13 states, "Then Jesus arrived from Galilee at the Jordan *coming* to John, to be baptized by him. 14 But John tried to prevent him;" (Matthew 3:13–14a).

Did you catch that? I am amazed how many times I have read this and missed that little phrase, "but John tried to prevent him." John tried to prevent Jesus from being baptized because it did not fit into his theological grid. John knows his purpose. He is to decrease. Jesus is to increase. It is the greater that baptizes the lesser. Something does not "seem" to be right.

John tells Jesus, "I have need to be baptized by you, and do you come to me?" (Matthew 3:14b). Many of us find ourselves in John's position. We were pretty sure of what our purpose was for the congregation that we are leading. We were sure that we knew what God wanted us to accomplish; however, if we listen closely, what we are recognizing is that God has placed a twist in his plan for us. It is not that we have not been faithful. We have. It is not that we were not following the Lord's leading. We were. It is that God has more to his agenda than he has previously shared with us. It may be time to slow down and listen to what God is saying regarding our ministry. What is God already doing? This may be the new direction that he wants from us.

Jesus tells John, "Permit *it* at this time; for in this way it is fitting for us to fulfill all righteousness." In other words, "John, I know this situation does not make sense to you right now, but I need you to follow my lead. It is time to twist. I am doing something that is bigger than your personal ministry. We're fulfilling all righteousness and you are the person I chose to help me with this task." (Matthew 3:15a)

The great part about this passage is that John obeyed. The text states, "Then he [*John*] permitted him." (Matthew 3:15b). John permitted Jesus to accomplish his work through him. I wonder how many times I have kept Jesus from accomplishing his work through our ministry and me because I had already made up my mind regarding what I was going to get accomplished for Jesus.

Because John was obedient to Jesus, he got to experience something unbelievably spectacular. Nowhere in Scripture does it say that John performed a miracle, but because of his obedience, he certainly got to experience one. The text says,

> 16 After being baptized, Jesus came up immediately from the water; and behold, the heavens were opened, and he saw the Spirit of God descending as a dove *and* lighting on him, 17 and behold, a voice out of the heavens said, 'This is My beloved Son, in whom I am well-pleased;[7]

Now, that's worth shouting about! Glory to God!

God is doing something extraordinary in your midst. The key is to ask God to show you what he is doing so that you can help your church align with his purpose for your church. It may be a twist from what you were doing, but it will be for a greater purpose than what you do "for him." As you begin to see God's work in your ministry, celebrate his faithfulness to your ministry. Twist and Shout!

---

7. Matthew 3:16–17.

6

You Are Not the Church

*"Keep your face to the sunshine
and you cannot see a shadow."*

—Helen Keller

In Kindergarten, we used to play a lot of crazy games. I remember playing the game called, "Tag." My kids play that same game. One person is labeled as "It," and that person has to try and tag someone else before they reach the safe area. Another game we used to play was "Hide and Go Seek." Once again, someone was designated as "It," but in this game others were given the opportunity to hide before the person designated as "It" could begin the process of looking for them. These games helped us to play with others and get exercise.

However, there was another game that I used to play that had very little purpose other than causing self-frustration. No one taught me this game. It was a game that I am sure other kids have played, but I have never asked. It is a game that I never won. Fortunately, I grew out of playing the game when I got older. The game is called, "Outrunning your shadow."

For some strange reason, I believed that I could out run or trick my shadow. With my feet on the ground, my goal was to separate myself from my shadow. I would run as fast as I could. I would move side to side as quickly as possible. I would turn around in circles. I would run backwards. Guess what? No matter what I did, I could not separate myself from my shadow. Finally, I realized it was a useless enterprise and I gave up the game.

Most adults don't pay attention to their shadow. We know that shadows are not really us. They exist because light is shining on us and where our body blocks the sunlight it leaves a shadow. Our shadow may be longer than our body or shorter. It may be wider or thinner. It may be distorted or perfectly aligned with our body. For the most part, our shadow is more dependent upon the light than our actual body. Although our shadow is with us every day, we pay very little attention to it. We know that our shadow is not really a part of us.

So why do we obsess about our church? It is true that in some way our church is constantly with us, just like a shadow, but it is *not us*. We have very little to do about the size, the health and the well-being of the people in our church. Don't get me wrong, I am not saying that we don't have an impact on these things. We do. However, we have no *control* over these things. We are to do the best we can to nurture our people in the fear and admonition of the Lord, but at the end of the day what happens is beyond our control.

Jesus stated in Matthew 16:18b, ". . . upon this rock I will build my church; and the gates of Hades will not overpower it." It is Jesus who is building his church, not us.

You Are Not the Church

Jesus said that he would build his church. Yes, we are to be good shepherds of the sheep. Yes, we are attached to our churches, but we should not be obsessing over them.

One of my students, who is also a pastor, shared with me that he was on the verge of burnout. He stated that he hadn't had a day off in months. I asked him why, and he told me that he couldn't afford to take a day off. It wasn't because of finances. It was because he was expected to meet the needs of the ministry seven days a week. My assignment for him was to begin working towards one day off per week. After the course ended, I saw him several months later at a leaders meeting. He shared that he was finally taking Fridays off and he was so glad he took my assignment seriously. He no longer felt burnout.

My parents' church was founded in 1926. On a wall, in a room, in the basement of the church, are a series of photographs. These pictures are the ten to fifteen pastors from the inception of the church. Very few people go down into the basement for the purpose of viewing these photographs. Very few people stop to read the names under each picture. Almost no one remembers what these individuals did. Unfortunately, these are just photos of dead, retired and forgotten men. If you are fortunate, this will be your legacy as well.

God wants us to be faithful to the ministry that he has given us. But we have to remember that he is building the church, not us. Make sure that you are taking time off to spend with the Lord and your family. Make sure that you are not burning the candle at both ends continually. At some point you have to trust God to do what you physically, emotionally, mentally and spiritually do not have the ability to accomplish in your own strength.

I love Psalm 127. Although it is usually seen as a lesson regarding home life, I believe it speaks especially to the pastor and his home life. Let's take a look at verse two, especially the last line.

> It is vain for you to rise up early, / To retire late, / To eat the bread of painful labors; / For He gives His beloved sleep. / [Or the last line could be] For He gives to His beloved even in his sleep.

The psalmist is stating the futility of burning the candle at both ends. At some point we have to trust God to make up the difference. The Hebrew is unclear as to whether the Lord will provide sleep for his beloved or provide for his beloved during his or her sleep. I think that the ambiguity is purposeful. I believe God provides both. If we trust him, he will give us our rest and he will build his church. Sweet dreams!

SABBATH REST

One of the things I want to share is the importance of pastors getting weekly rest. This is not a debate on whether or not Sabbath rest in the Scriptures is still in effect. I know there are people who have different views on this topic, but this has to do with the way God has created us.

I believe God has created us to rest one day a week. Not only do I believe this is Biblically supported, but I believe the scientific and business community also supports this. I'll give you two examples:

A number of years ago in the *Wall Street Journal*, there was an article about an individual who had just passed away and he had spent his life living in caves.[1] Not because he was a caveman, but because this was something that he enjoyed doing. He would live in the caves for months, sometimes years. One of the things the scientists would do

---

1. Miller and Berretta, "He Traded Company for Caves To Study Effects of Isolation," *Wall Street Journal*.

You Are Not the Church

is wire him and monitor his bodily functions while he was underground. He would be underground and have no recollection of when it was day or night, did not have a clock and was unaware of the seasons. One of the things the scientists noticed was that even though he did not consciously know what was going on outside the cave, they were able to "confirm longer biological cycles, for instance the 'circaseptan,' a weeklong period during which certain biological functions resolve."[2] It was like clockwork. It appears that every seven days, we need a reset, and that seems to align with the Sabbath rest that God wants us to have.

Also, a number of years ago, *Harvard Business Review* did a study of high-powered consultants that worked seven days a week.[3] The consultants were required to take one day off per week, and to their surprise, the team members were more efficient and the consulting team was more productive as a result of this process. The article states, "The work became better integrated because people were interacting better and more often. Inevitably, this led to improvements in the quality of work delivered—benefits that were certainly noticed by clients."[4]

I believe that Sabbath rest is really a gift from God to us. It is not about legalism or trying to keep some type of law. God knows how he created us, and he did it in such a way that when we spend a day of reflection, rest and recovery, it gives us the ability to be able to work much more efficiently in the six days following. In the experiment noted in the *Harvard Business Review*, one consultant stated, "My project manager pushed me out of the office to make sure I took the time off . . . even though it was a busy week. I

2. Ibid.

3. Perlow and Porter, "Making Time Off Predictable—and Required," *Harvard Business Review,* 102–109.

4. Ibid., 108.

came back really refreshed."[5] What is interesting in the two previous examples is that neither included God.

I believe from a Christian perspective that God *gives to his beloved even in his sleep,* and the health of God's church does not depend on the pastor. It is really dependent on God. You are not the church.

PRACTICAL APPLICATIONS

Here are some ideas to help ensure that your Sabbath rest is productive and rewarding:

- Don't confuse a worship service on the Sabbath with having your own personal Sabbath.
- Don't use that day as sermon or teaching preparation. If you do read the Bible, read it for personal enrichment.
- Choose a day other than Sunday for rest.
- Determine what you consider work activities and consciously choose not to do those on your Sabbath day.
- Choose to engage in activities that refresh your soul (These things can be recreational, hobbies, sports, gardening, etc . . .).
- Block out that time on your calendar—don't let anything invade that time!
- Let others know that this is your day of rest/refreshment. Treat it as an appointment with God.
- Expect "urgent but unimportant"[6] requests to try and invade your Sabbath time.
- Use the day to reconnect with God.

5. Ibid., 105.

6. This phrase was used by Stephen Covey in his book, *First Things First.*

7

Mirror, Mirror, On the Wall . . .[1]

As pastors of small churches, we need to realize that pastors of large churches are not our enemy. I have never met a large-church pastor who views pastors of small churches as his enemy. What I *have* run into is a number of small-church pastors who think that large-church pastors are against them, antagonistic toward them, or their rivals. Oftentimes, I will hear that the reason our churches are smaller is that we are holding to the truth and purity of the Word. In turn we look at churches that are exploding numerically and think that they must be doing something wrong. They must not be preaching the *pure* Word of the Gospel. That may be true for some churches, but not for all. I would say that the majority of large evangelical churches and pastors that I know *are* preaching and teaching the Word. And God, for his own reasons and purposes, has chosen to bless their ministry numerically.

We have to make sure that we are not like the queen in the fairy tale, Snow White, who constantly asks the magic

1. Rickard and Blank, *Snow White and the Seven Dwarfs*, Walt Disney Studios.

mirror, "Mirror, mirror, on the wall, who's the fairest of them all?"[2] The queen thought she was better and more deserving of the acclaim and it caused her to become envious and vindictive. When we react inappropriately to the things that we talked about earlier in this book (depression, discouragement, and disillusionment), it is easy for us to view the churches that are growing exponentially as the enemy. That is the furthest thing from the truth. The truth is that we are all part of the body of Christ.

When we look carefully at the last chapter in the book of Romans, we realize that when Paul is writing to the Church of Rome, he is writing to a number of different churches that meet in different locations. But yet, he views them all as the body of Christ (see Romans 16:3–5, 10, 11, 14, 15).[3]

I want to suggest this: As opposed to viewing large churches as being our enemy, what we need to do is build partnerships with these churches. One of the blessings regarding large churches is their abundant resources; they are able to do a number of things that small churches are not able to do. And yet, if we were to work with them or approach them and suggest that we do joint activities together, we may find that they are very open to that. For example, there are a number of large churches in our region that organize and lead short-term mission trips, summer camps and other ministerial training. What we've done is approach those churches and asked, "Can we partner with what you are already doing?" I have never been turned down.

Also, I understand that there may be a concern regarding losing members when we do something like that.

2. Ibid.

3. Many view Paul as writing to as many as five difference churches.

Mirror, Mirror, On the Wall . . .

We have not lost anyone due to a joint ministry project. In fact, it is an encouragement to our people that we can do the same projects as larger churches. Each project has been a great opportunity for the body of Christ to work together to do something that benefitted both ministries. I want to suggest that we begin working with larger churches and we stop viewing them as the enemy. As the great philosopher Pogo once stated, "We have met the enemy and he is us."[4]

Not only should we begin working with larger churches, but we should also begin working with parachurch organizations. There are a number of good ministries doing a lot of good work; inner city ministries, global ministries, and international ministries. All we need to do is begin a dialogue with them to see what things they are already doing. There is a great possibility that we can come alongside and help them, while in turn they also help us. Our church has been able to support missions and/or missionaries on every continent (except Antarctica). We have not been able to do it to the same extent that the larger churches have, but we have been able to continually support missions and missionaries around the globe. This has been a real blessing. People are surprised that a smaller church has been able accomplish all that we have. The president of one local mission told me that their main supporter was a large megachurch in the area. However, the second largest contributor to their mission was our church. Isn't that awesome? It doesn't really matter the size of the church, it is a matter of the vision. Are we going to do what God has called us to do no matter what our size?

I want to suggest as well that we look at some of the new movements that are happening especially in America. In the Detroit-Metropolitan area, one of the things we have going at the time of this writing is Everyone a Chance to

---

4. Kelly, *Pogo: We Have Met The Enemy and He Is Us,* 1987.

Pastoring the Small Church

Hear (E.A.C.H.), where a number of churches and parachurch ministries in southeastern Michigan are working together to try and reach this region for Jesus Christ. This is a wonderful opportunity for churches to become involved in reaching their community with other churches in their area. A similar thing is going on in Milwaukee called "Rock the Lakes," where a number of churches regionally are working together to reach the region. Kevin Palau is leading a movement out of Portland, Oregon called "Season of Service." Currently, there are pockets of churches and parachurch organizations joining together to do great things in the community. This is a wonderful opportunity for small-church pastors to stop asking, "are we the fairest of them all?" and to join with other like-minded believers to reach their community for Jesus Christ.

In 2 Corinthians chapter 9, we find Paul addressing the Corinthian believers regarding preparing a gift for the churches of Macedonia. He instructs them to support one another even if it is just monetarily. Here Paul states,

> 5 So I thought it necessary to urge the brethren that they would go on ahead to you and arrange beforehand your previously promised bountiful gift, so that the same would be ready as a bountiful gift and not affected by covetousness. 6 Now this *I say*, he who sows sparingly will also reap sparingly, and he who sows bountifully will also reap bountifully. 7 Each one *must do* just as he has purposed in his heart, not grudgingly or under compulsion, for God loves a cheerful giver. 8 And God is able to make all grace abound to you, so that always having all sufficiency in everything, you may have an abundance for every good deed; 9 as it is written, "He scattered abroad, he gave to the poor, his righteousness endures forever."10 Now He who supplies seed

Mirror, Mirror, On the Wall . . .

> to the sower and bread for food will supply and multiply your seed for sowing and increase the harvest of your righteousness; 11 you will be enriched in everything for all liberality, which through us is producing thanksgiving to God. 12 For the ministry of this service is not only fully supplying the needs of the saints, but is also overflowing through many thanksgivings to God;

Paul had sent men ahead of him to remind and prepare a financial gift for the church of Jerusalem. Paul expected churches to work together for the benefit of the kingdom. He expected the Corinthians to help the poor in Jerusalem. However, this was not just a requirement placed upon the Corinthian church.

In the fifteenth chapter of the Book of Romans, the apostle Paul is explaining his travel plans to the churches in Rome. He plans to stop by Rome on his way to Spain. However, he needs to make a stop in Jerusalem first. He explains the reason for his Jerusalem trip and his expectations of those in Rome. He states,

> 24 Whenever I go to Spain—for I hope to see you in passing, and to be helped on my way there by you, when I have first enjoyed your company for a while— 25 but now, I am going to Jerusalem serving the saints. 26 For Macedonia and Achaia have been pleased to make a contribution for the poor among the saints in Jerusalem. 27 Yes, they were pleased *to do so*, and they are indebted to them. For if the Gentiles have shared in their spiritual things, they are indebted to minister to them also in material things;

Paul is in the process of taking a financial gift to the church of Jerusalem. When Paul refers to Achaia, he is probably referring to the Corinthian church. Paul explains that not only were the churches of Macedonia and Achaia pleased to contribute a gift, but they were indebted to do so. In similar fashion, Paul expects to be "helped" by the Roman believers as he passes by on his way to Spain. It is clear that we are to help one another for the cause of Christ.

Although, these examples do not show churches physically coming together to complete a project, they do show support for one another. What is interesting in this first century example is who is helping who? It appears that the smaller churches are working together to help the larger church in Jerusalem. What a novel idea?

8

Delight Yourself in the Lord

"Always borrow money from a pessimist;
he doesn't expect to be paid back."

—Author Unknown

One of my favorite summer past times is growing a vegetable garden. The assortment of vegetables may consist of cucumbers, tomatoes, summer squash and zucchini. Every now and then, someone will give me advice on how to grow larger produce. Each time I've tried these tidbits of wisdom, I have ruined my vegetables. It is not that I don't appreciate the advice; it is just that no one knows the complex composition of my soil like me.

It seems that everyone has some tidbits of wisdom in how to grow a large church as well. One of the most perplexing philosophies of our current Christian culture is the obsession with the large church. The spotlight seems to shine on these behemoths of the Christian community. As a result, the small church and its faithful pastor unintentionally get left in the shadows. Yet, the Apostle Paul makes it clear in 1 Corinthians 4:2, that it is a requirement of [*God's*] steward that he is found faithful, not that he lead a large congregation.

I understand that some may feel that leading a small church can be drudgery. However, it does not have to be. I believe that faithfully leading a small church can be a joy. I have had the opportunity to travel to Uganda and Haiti during the last couple of years. One of the most remarkable things that I have found is that believers who don't have as many material goods as we do in the United States *seem* to have more joy. This has not only been my observation, but the observations of others who have served in short term or long term missions in third world countries.[1] For example, David Platt refers to an email sent to him from one such believer:

> "The man decided this word about God was too good to keep to himself. So he writes me from Uganda, where he is teaching the doctrine of God to church members and leaders there. He is not a staff member or a paid minister; he is simply a man in love with God's Word. He writes, 'Pastor, for ten hours a day, I am preaching my heart out by his grace! We have sat for hours talking through the Word, and God has spoken with such a mighty hand of truth that I can't even begin to tell you about it all now! Praise the glorious name of Christ—he is being exalted a continent away!'"[2]

Platt also shares about a Christian in India, who under adverse conditions still exudes joy. He states, "One Christian in India, while being skinned alive, looked at his persecutors

---

1. This is qualitative, not quantitative.
2. David Platt, *Radical*, 41.

Delight Yourself in the Lord

and said, 'I thank you for this. Tear off my old garment, for I will soon put on Christ's garment of righteousness.'"[3] I often wonder why believers in third-world countries can express this type of joy? Could it be that with the absence of this world's goods and prestige, there is more reason to focus on a relationship with Jesus Christ?

Most of us would agree that being the pastor of a small church brings little prestige and few of this world's goods. Could leading a small church be a source of real joy?

Andy Stanley, in an article in *Leadership Journal*,[4] stated that the best analogy of a contemporary pastor is a CEO rather than a shepherd. I totally understand his reasoning and to a certain extent agree when it comes to the large church. The size of the church and the layers of management needed to run a large organization keeps a pastor from being intricately involved in the lives of his people. He has to run it like a CEO.

However, this is not the case with the pastor of a small church. The pastor of a small church knows all of his people by name. He knows the spiritual health of all his members. He knows how to pray for each of the parents regarding their children. Depending on his length of service, he may have been at the hospital when a child was born, baptized that same child, officiated her wedding when she grew up and performed her father's funeral. It is a family affair. In some ways, every person in the church is part of his extended family.

In the small church, it is not about meeting certain metrics, but living among God's people. Although you may only baptize one person this year, that person was Susan, whose story you know very well. It is remarkable that Susan is even alive. Although there is only one person in the

3. Ibid., 35.
4. Interview with Andy Stanley, "State of the Art," *Leadership*, 27.

congregation with cancer, everyone in the church is praying for Tommy. The church can't imagine living without him. Although there is only one person getting married this year, the entire church is invited. It is going to be a great time. What a joy!

These days there is a lot of information about the benefits of small group ministry. Visit any Christian bookstore and you can find a book or DVD explaining the "how" and "why" of small groups. The main focus is community. This is not a concern in the small church. The small church is in essence a larger small group. Everyone knows everyone and is concerned about everyone. You could say the solution to small groups is the small church.

I am not saying that small churches are better than the large churches. However, I am not saying that the large church is better than the smaller ones either. I am saying that each church is unique and that pastoring either church is what you make it. Gary McIntosh states in his book, *One Size Doesn't Fit All*, "There are three basic sizes of churches—small, medium, and large. While all churches resemble some aspects of all sizes of churches, each one demonstrates specific characteristics based on the category of size it falls into."[5]

One of my favorite people in scripture is Anna. We meet Anna in the second chapter of the Gospel of Luke. The text states,

> 36 And there was a prophetess, Anna the daughter of Phanuel, of the tribe of Asher. She was advanced in years and had lived with her husband seven years after her marriage, 37 and then as a widow to the age of eighty-four. She never left the temple, serving night and day with fasting and prayers. 38 At that very moment she came up

---

5. McIntosh, *One Size Doesn't Fit All*, 21.

Delight Yourself in the Lord

and began giving thanks to God, and continued to speak of him to all those who were looking for the redemption of Jerusalem;

Each time I read this passage, I think to myself, "Anna got a raw deal." She is a prophetess during New Testament times. There is a good possibility that she was not in the inner circle of the religious establishment. The Pharisees generally viewed women with contempt.[6] She was probably tolerated rather than greatly respected.

Her genealogy was not impressive: she was from the tribe of Asher, which was one of the apostate northern tribes that was judged by God and destroyed by Assyria.

She was married for seven years before her husband died. The text does not say why she did not marry again. It could have been due to her commitment to the Lord. However, it could have been that nobody wanted to marry her after her husband's death and she remained a widow. If her husband had an unmarried brother, it would have been his responsibility to marry her in order to raise up a child in her husband's name.[7] If this was the case, it obviously did not happen.

If she was married around the average age that young women were married in the New Testament, she was approximately sixteen years of age.[8] This means that Anna spent approximately sixty-one years in the Temple with little recognition or influence. Yet, she is mentioned in Scripture right along with Jesus, Joseph, Mary and Simeon.

---

6. In the Talmud, it states, "It was taught: R. Judah used to say, A man is bound to say the following three blessings daily: '[Blessed art thou . . .] who hast not made me a heathen', ' . . . who hast not made me a woman'; and ' . . . who hast not made me a brutish man.' " *Talmud;* Menahoth 43b–44a.

7. Deuteronomy 25:5–10.

8. Balch and Osiek, *Early Christian Families in Context*, 140.

How is it that a culturally insignificant servant of Yahweh is mentioned in the birth narrative of Jesus Christ? It was because she was faithful.

I often wonder what the story would have been if Anna had only been faithful sixty years instead of sixty-one. What if she had made up her mind that "If significance doesn't come by the sixtieth year, I am outta here!"? Would the text say, "And here is where Anna would have thanked God for Jesus, but she quit being faithful due to her lack of feeling significant. That is too bad for poor Anna."

You are not insignificant in your ministry. The Lord sees your faithfulness. You may not be noticed or viewed as significant by the world (Christian or secular), but you are extremely valuable to God. You are a key part of His program. Rejoice, O servant of God! Give thanks! Delight yourself in the Lord! And continue speaking of Jesus to all who are looking for redemption. You are significant to God!

9

Bring the Rain

"If you count all the things you don't have, you'll never get to the end of the list."

—Mike Stoddard

When I was a kid, almost every summer my family would travel by car from Detroit, Michigan to Pine Bluff, Arkansas. Those were the days when cars did not have air conditioning. The only cool breeze available on our trip was when we were traveling at high speeds in the evenings. Most of the trip, my brother and I were roasting in the back seat. If that wasn't bad enough, there was not a great selection of radio stations. Either we listened to music with static in the background or to local music, which sounded foreign to my urban ears. We filled our travel time by playing a game called "Ford® Mustang." We would look down the highway and the first family member to see and yell, "Mustang" got a point. The person with the most points would win the game. The game would detract us from our miserableness for a while. However, after a few minutes, even "Mustang" couldn't mask the fact that the trip was horrible. Even as I write this, I feel that I need to apologize to my parents for the number of times I asked, "Are we there yet?" The only thing that made the journey bearable was the knowledge that eventually I would see my grandmother. Seeing and talking with her was the highlight of my summer. Although my grandmother had eighteen grandchildren, each of us always felt like we were extremely special to her. The pain of the ride was all but forgotten when I saw Grandma. Grandma was worth the ride.

For many small church pastors, their experience in ministry is probably like my ride "down south." The present journey is pretty miserable. The one overriding hope is that when they see Jesus it will be well worth the journey. Let me concur. I believe that will be the case. I believe that when we see Jesus, all of our problems, heartaches and pains will quickly dissolve into the background and our joy will be so overwhelming that everything that came before will be insignificant in comparison. I believe I have biblical support for this view. Even the Apostle Paul stated that in Romans 8:18, "For I consider that the sufferings of this present time are not worthy to be compared with the glory that is to be revealed to us." So that is a great comfort, the ultimate comfort. But is it the only comfort?

My answer is "not necessarily." There is a great possibility that God wants to do great things in your present ministry. These great things might depend on seeing what God is already doing and getting on board with the program. The writer of the letter to the Hebrews states, the following in chapter six,

> 9 But, beloved, we are convinced of better things concerning you, and things that accompany salvation, though we are speaking in this way;

Bring the Rain

After warning the Hebrews of the dangers of falling away from the faith, he tells them that he is convinced of "better things" concerning them. Exactly what are these better things? A couple of verses earlier give us a clue. He states,

> 7 For ground that drinks the rain which often falls on it and brings forth vegetation useful to those for whose sake it is also tilled, receives a blessing from God;

The "better thing" is the ground that absorbs the rain and produces a bountiful crop and receives a blessing from God. The lesser thing is in verse 8,

> 8 But if it yields thorns and thistles, it is worthless and close to being cursed, and it ends up being burned.

The lesser thing would be the ground that does not bring forth vegetation, but rather weeds. The best that can be done is to set the field on fire and hope that something worthwhile will grow next year.

Now let us look back at Hebrews 6:9–10,

> 9 But, beloved, we are convinced of better things concerning you, and things that accompany salvation, though we are speaking in this way. 10 For God is not unjust so as to forget your work and the love which you have shown toward His name, in having ministered and in still ministering to the saints;

The writer to the Hebrews is expecting great things from these believers. He wants to encourage them to remain faithful to what God has called them. God will not forget the labor that they have put into the ministry.

One of the wonderful things about this passage is that it is written to a predominantly Jewish congregation of believers in Jesus Christ. These believers are encouraged to continue on in their faith. However, if we dissect the previous passage, we might ask the question, "Who is providing the rain?" Certainly it is God, but "By what means is God providing it?" Is he not providing it by the preacher of God who continues faithfully to share the Word week in and week out? Is not the preacher providing the same rain on the soil of the hearts of these believers? He is not only ministering to the saints, but he is also distributing the rain.

In the Book of Revelation, there is a phrase that often gets overlooked. Revelation 1:3 states,

> Blessed is he who reads and those who hear the words of the prophecy, and heed the things which are written in it; for the time is near;

There are three actions that are blessed in this verse: reading, hearing and heeding. Often they are taken as three separate activities. However, I believe that they are best to be seen as two separate activities. There is the reading, and then there is the hearing and heeding (or acting upon what is being heard). In our contemporary culture we might think that there is no difference in reading and hearing. We might think this because we live in literate culture where everyone can have a copy of the Scriptures. However, in the time of this letter, there were not many copies and not everyone had the ability to read. So there are actually blessings on two types of individuals, not three. In other words, "blessed are the individuals who read the word of God out loud so that others may hear and obey." "And blessed are those who hear and obey." The communicator of God's word is in the wonderful position of being blessed twice.[1]

---

1. "Studies of literacy in the ancient Mediterranean world place the number of people who could read, write, or do both at somewhere around 5 percent, rising to perhaps as high as 15 percent for urban males . . . we need to recognize that the written texts were

I see a similar thing in Hebrews, chapter six. Not only will God not forget our service unto him, but also he gives us this wonderful privilege to be the disseminator of his word.

All he asks is what is in Hebrews 6:11–12,

> 11 And we desire that each one of you show the same diligence so as to realize the full assurance of hope until the end, 12 so that you will not be sluggish, but imitators of those who through faith and patience inherit the promises.

God wants us to remain diligent unto the end. Anyone who knows his Bible is familiar with chapter eleven of the Book of Hebrews. It is considered by some as the Hall of Faith. Here the Hebrew writer lists several individuals who have lived by faith. None of these individuals were perfect. Some got to receive earthly rewards after a life of trusting God. Others lived their entire life without embracing rewards on this side of eternity. However all of them will inherit the promises in eternity.

I believe this is what the writer is alluding to here in chapter six. This is the application for us as well. We who are the disseminators of God's Word are to remain faithful. God will reward our efforts, maybe in this lifetime, but definitely in the life to come.

Remain faithful.

---

relatively few, those responsible for the creation of these written texts less than a handful of the population . . . " in Horsley, Draper and Foley, *Performing the Gospel,* 18–19.

Epilogue

"I think we've all arrived at a very special place. Spiritually, ecumenically, grammatically."

—CAPTAIN JACK SPARROW[1]

I BELIEVE IT WAS one of my seminary professors that said, "Most people love to talk about their convictions, but very few will die for them." I hope this is not true. I especially hope that this is not true with regards to God's shepherds. There are some things that we should be willing to die for. I think I can safely say that a few of those things are: The Deity of Jesus Christ, the doctrine of the Trinity and the purity of the gospel. However, I wonder if there are other things that are not as important, but are worth holding onto for dear life? In fact, it may cost us our spiritual life if we don't hold on to them. I believe some of those things are the principles I have discussed in this book.

    I have concluded that my spiritual life depends upon these things. I have realized that if I don't guard my heart, nobody else is going to guard it for me. I will die. It will be a slow death. It will not be apparent to the casual observer. It will be a lonely death. I'll probably be the only one who

---

1. Elliott and Rossio, *Pirates of the Caribbean,* Walt Disney Studios.

knows I am dying. It will be a bitter death. I will hate the day that I was called into ministry. However, make no mistake; it will be death to my soul.

I believe that a number of small church pastors are dying a little bit every day. When they began in the pastorate, their spiritual life was an oasis of vitality. Now it has come to resemble the cracked earth of a field in the midst of severe drought. It does not have to be that way. The insights that I have shared in this book have helped me to navigate the deep blue seas of being a small church pastor.

The main character in the *Pirates of the Caribbean*[2] movies is Captain Jack Sparrow. Captain Jack is a unique individual. He is a sailor and a pirate at heart. However, due to some misfortune, he has lost his ship, The Black Pearl. A major theme throughout the movies is Jack's quest to reclaim control of the Black Pearl. Each scene of each movie that involves Captain Jack is a new adventure. Although I cannot endorse Captain Jack's morals, I can appreciate his love of adventure on the open seas.

So pastors, grab your compass. Lift the anchor. Hoist the sails, for I am confident that the principles in this book will help you navigate your way through the stormy seas of small church ministry.

Happy Sailing!

2. Ibid.

Bibliography

Amundsen, Darrel W. "The Anguish and Agonies of Charles Spurgeon." *Christian History*, Issue 29, Volume X, No. 1, 23–35.

Balch, David L. and Carolyn Osiek. *Early Christian Families in Context: An Interdisciplinary Dialogue*. Grand Rapids: Eerdmans, 2003.

Beeke, Joel R. and Terry D. Slachter. *Encouragement for Today's Pastor: Help from the Puritans*. Grand Rapids: Reformation Heritage, 2013.

Bierly, Steve R. *Help for the Small-Church Pastor: Unlocking the Potential of Your Congregation*. Grand Rapids: Zondervan, 1995.

Bierly, Steve R. *How to Thrive as a Small Church Pastor: A Guide to Spiritual and Emotional Well-Being*. Grand Rapids: Zondervan, 1998.

Boa, Kenneth. *Conformed to His Image*. Grand Rapids: Zondervan, 2001.

Callahan, Kennon L. *Small, Strong Congregations: Creating Strengths and Health for Your Congregation*. San Francisco: Jossey-Bass Inc., 2000.

Chu, Lenora. "Priced to grow: How Costco got started," *CNN Money*. http://money.cnn.com/2009/08/14/smallbusiness/how_costco_got_started.fsb/index.htm.

Coote, Robert B. *Mustard Seed Churches: Ministries in Small Churches*. Minneapolis: Fortress, 1990.

Covey, Stephen R., A. Roger Merrill, and Rebecca R. Merrill. *First Things First*. Great Britain: Simon & Schuster, 1994.

Daman, Glenn C. *Shepherding the Small Church*. Grand Rapids: Kregel Academic & Professional, 2002.

Dudley, Carl S. *Effective Small Churches in the Twenty-First Century*. Nashville: Abingdon Press, 2003.

Elliott, Ted and Rossio, Terry. *Pirates of the Caribbean: The Curse of the Black Pearl,* directed by Gore Verbinski. Burbank, CA: Walt Disney Studios Home Entertainment, 2003.

Bibliography

Fuller, Jim. "10 Reasons Why Pastors Leave the Ministry." Pastoral Care, Inc. http://www.pastoralcareinc.com/articles/10-reasons-why-ministers-quit/.

Graves, A. "The Best Jobs of 2012: The Year's hottest jobs are hiring in droves, paying well, and providing room to grow," US News and World Report, http://money.usnews.com/money/careers/articles/2012/02/27/the-best-jobs-of-2012.

Hawkins, Greg L. and Cally Parkinson. *Move: What 1,000 Churches Reveal About Spiritual Growth*. Grand Rapids: Zondervan, 2011.

Hayes, Isaac and Porter, David. "Soul Man." Sam & Dave, *Soul Men*, Atlantic Records, 1967.

Home Depot®, *Our Company: History*. Home Depot. https://corporate.homedepot.com/OurCompany/History/Pages/default.aspx

Horsley, Richard A., Jonathan M. Draper, and John Miles Foley. *Performing the Gospel: Orality, Memory, and Mark*. Minneapolis: Fortress, 2006.

Hulse, Erroll and David Kingdon, eds. *A Marvelous Ministry: How the All-round Ministry of Charles Haddon Spurgeon Speaks to us Today*. Ligonier, PA: Soli Deo Gloria, 1993.

Junger, Sebastian. *The Perfect Storm: A True Story of Men Against the Sea*. New York: W. W. Norton & Company, 1997. This story was also made into a movie in the year 2000: *The Perfect Storm*, DVD, directed by Wolfgang Petersen. 2000; Burbank, CA: Warner Home Video, 2004.

Kelly, Walt. *Pogo: We Have Met The Enemy and He Is Us*. New York: Simon & Schuster, 1987.

Leadership Interview with Andy Stanley. "State of the Art: Negotiating the New Straits: Business models and Church Expectations," *Leadership* Spring 2006.

Maranatha Life's Life-Line For Pastors, "Statistics About Pastors," Maranatha Life, http://maranathalife.com/lifeline/stats.htm

McIntosh, Gary. *One Size Doesn't Fit All: Bringing Out the Best in Any Church Size*. Grand Rapids: Baker, 1999.

Medley, Phil and Bret Burns. "Twist and Shout," The Beatles, *Please Please Me,* London: Abbey Road Studios, 1963.

Miller, Stephen and Davide Berretta. "He Traded Company for Caves To Study Effects of Isolation." *Wall Street Journal*, September 22, 2009.

Olson, David T. *The American Church in Crisis*. Grand Rapids, MI: Zondervan, 2008.

Pastoral Care, Inc., "Statistics in the Ministry," Pastoral Care, Inc., http://www.pastoralcareinc.com/statistics/.

Bibliography

Perlow, Leslie A. and Jessica L. Porter. "Making Time Off Predictable—and Required," *Harvard Business Review.* October, 2009: 102-109.

Platt, David. *Radical: Taking Back Your Faith from the American Dream.* Colorado Springs: Multnomah Books, 2010.

Ray, David R. *The Indispensable Guide for Smaller Churches.* Cleveland, OH: The Pilgrim Press, 2009.

Redding, Otis. "RESPECT," Aretha Franklin, *I Never Loved a Man The Way I Love You,* New York: Atlantic Records, 1967.

Rickard, Dick and Blank, Dorothy Ann. 1937. *Snow White and the Seven Dwarfs.* Directed by Ben Sharpsteen, David Hand, Larry Morey, Perce Pearce, and Wilfred Jackson. Burbank, CA: Walt Disney Studios Home Entertainment.

Rima, Samuel D. 2002. *Rethinking the Successful Church: Finding Serenity in God's Sovereignty.* Grand Rapids: Baker Books.

Sam's Club®, *About Us: History.* Sam's Club®. http://www3.samsclub.com/NewsRoom/AboutUs/History

Talmud; Menahoth 43b-44a.

Thumma, Scott and Travis, Dave. Beyond Megachurch Myths: What we can learn from America's Largest Churches. San Francisco: Jossey-Bass.

Tucker, Ruth A. 2006. *Left Behind in a Megachurch World: How God Works through Ordinary Churches.* Grand Rapids: Baker Books.

Whitfield, Norman and Strong, Barrett. "I Heard It Through the Grapevine," Marvin Gaye, *In the Groove,* Detroit: Motown Records, 1968.

Willimon, William H. and Robert L. Wilson. *Preaching and Worship in the Small Church.* Nashville: Abingdon, 2002.

www.ingramcontent.com/pod-product-compliance
Lightning Source LLC
Chambersburg PA
CBHW051704090426
42736CB00013B/2527